EUPHORIC ATARAXIA

THE RHYTHMS OF A SPIRIT.

OMEGA

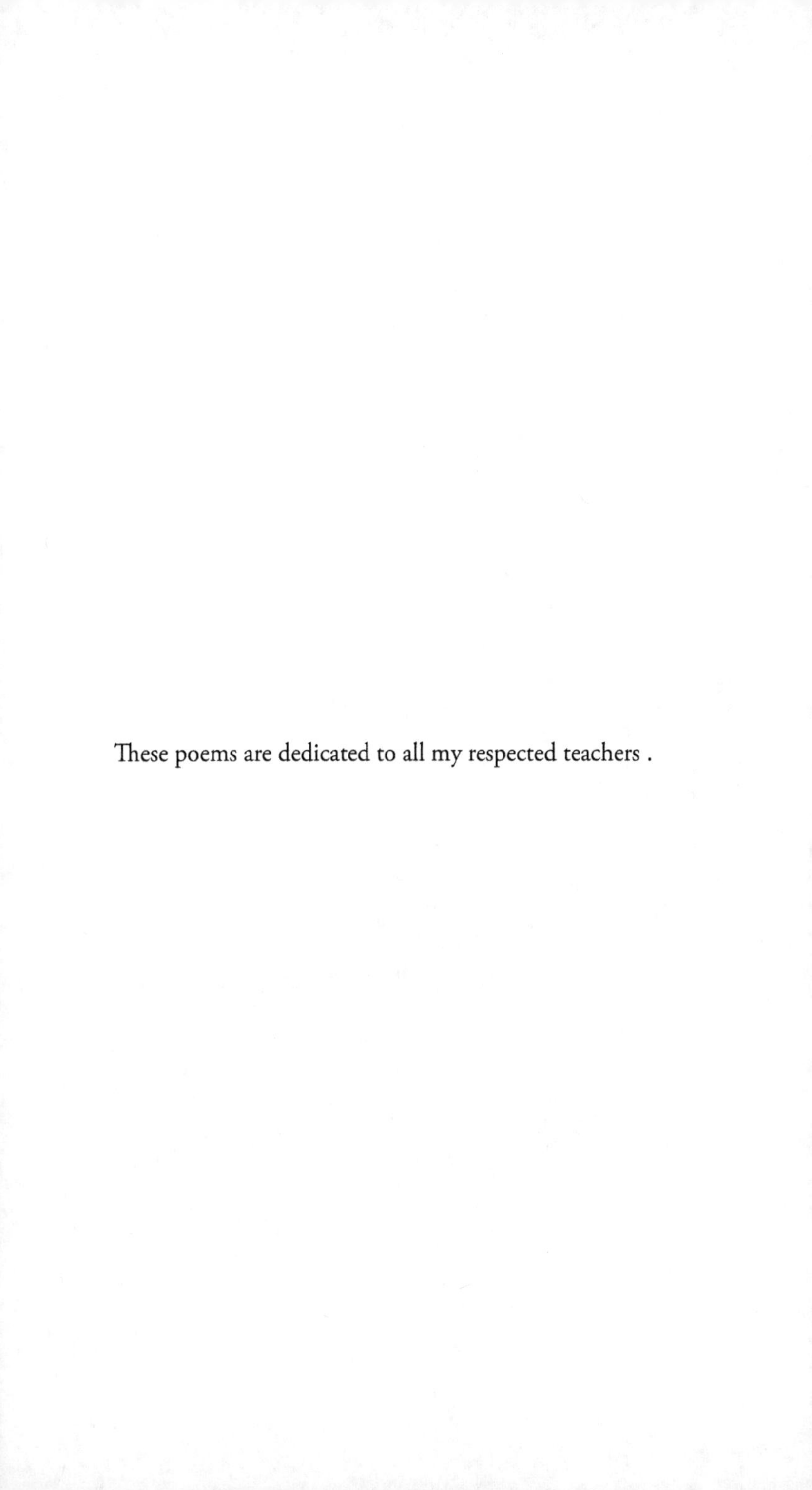

These poems are dedicated to all my respected teachers .

Contents

1. INSECURITIES

"Should i pull my mask,
should i not?
But i'm sure diving in a thought.
Sleeping eyes
awake when it cries,
because monsters are scaring
if you aren't so daring
to face them and look into their eyes
until you shed blood tears or,
make them end your fear."

2. NEW ERA

"Distant oceans , walking waves,
i find myself glowing in the shades.
Once again i feel retrieved,
once again i feel like mine.
But it's for the first time,
i'm not trying to shine.
As so far i've been
the brightest star
with the darkest scar."

3. RANDOM THOUGHTS 1

"Silence but voice,

suicide but choice.

All makes sense

until i'm not looking with my lens."

4. RANDOM THOUGHTS 2

"Casual talks,
silent walks.
I don't mind
to be lonely but kind."

5. GUTS

"This makes no sense
when you drop the chance
to lift your kneels up
and say shut your mouth up!"

6. AFRAID TO LOSE MYSELF

"Dark secrets creep inside
as the knife hits the doorside.
Praying to the god to become alive,
they still couldn't escape the dive
into a world full of surprises,
and where there lives were in crisis."

7. SUICIDE

As she exhaled a deep breath
she saw the coming death.
wrong choice seemed right
deep darkness replaced the light
blood droopo

8. HOPELESS

"No thought no matter,
no eyes no water.
Still maniac with depression,
in the middle of reality
and illusions."

9. MY BESTIE

"Blazing sunshine meets air,
while both of us heat with no care.
Through the window we enjoy the nature,
as our shadows lie on the furniture."

10. LITTLE THINGS

"I wish my sister
ALL THE BEST,
TOUCH THE CREST!
To my surprise
she replies ,
TOUCH THE TROUGH
and i cough!"

11. LETHARGIC

"Is it bad,

to be bad?

Spending all night and day in my bed.

I'm sad cause i don't have anything to share.

I'm mad

on myself,

cause i have no reasons to care.

But i feel glad

that you are not here,

to see the blood

scattered everywhere."

12. SERIOUS

"Sometimes i think how can i die?
Someimes i think how can i cry?
If they are always standing beside me,
not knowing that i could ever be free,
from all the anxiety i hold quietly
flooding inside violently.
I still try to blame myself everynight,
thinking about suicide
and their sacrifice
to keep me alive
at any price."

13. SLITS AND SLEEVES

"I left my consciousness
as i took the fine blade,
then swept the sleeves in sadness
as i cried in that dark shade."

14. BED OF BLADES

"My dreams weigh heavy
while i'm sleeping deadly,
and thinking whether or not
i should bury the thought
of slitting myself again
to let out the inner pain."

15. PARANORMAL

"Some voices i hear,
barely knowing if they're real.
Existence of two worls in same universe
is both a blessing and a curse.
You can teleport from here to there
to make either peace or destruction everywhere."

www.ingramcontent.com/pod-product-compliance
Lightning Source LLC
Chambersburg PA
CBHW071259140726
47996CB00007B/2907